DARK SQUARE

DARK SQUARE

Peter Marcus

Pleasure Boat Studio: A Literary Press
New York

Dark Square
Poems by Peter Marcus ©2012

ISBN 978-1-929355-82-2
Library of Congress Control Number: 2011942148
Design by Jason Schneiderman
Cover art: "The Lions of Coyoacán"/"Los leones de Coyoacán," c. 1929, by Manuel Alvarez Bravo. © Colette Urbajtel/ Archivo Bravo, SC

Pleasure Boat Studio books are available through the following:
SPD (Small Press Distribution) Tel. 800-869-7553, Fax 510-524-0852
Partners/West Tel. 425-227-8486, Fax 425-204-2448
Baker & Taylor 800-775-1100, Fax 800-775-7480
Ingram Tel 615-793-5000, Fax 615-287-5429
Amazon.com and bn.com

and through
PLEASURE BOAT STUDIO: A LITERARY PRESS
www.pleasureboatstudio.com
201 West 89th Street
New York, NY 10024

Contact Jack Estes
Fax; 888-810-5308
Email: pleasboat@nyc.rr.com

ACKNOWLEDGMENTS

ÄGNI: "The Insomniac's Pet Shop," "To Hear the Chorus Sing"
Bellevue Literary Review: "Doctor, Please"
Connecticut Review: "Courage," "Leaving Park Street Station"
Cream City Review: "The Water and the Glass that Contains It"
Green Mountains Review: "My Sister's Girlfriend"
Harvard Review: "Backseat"
Iowa Review: "The Affair," "Rodin Exhibit on the Rooftop,
        Metropolitan Museum of Art"
Kestrel: "Canvas & Distance"
Mudfish: "Blackberry Nights"
Negative Capability: "My Mother's Miscarriages"
New England Review: "Cutters," "The Embrace," "Dark Remedies"
North American Review: "Swans, Penguins, Whales & Us"
Notre Dame Review: "Tasco Triptych," "The Accordion Players"
Pivot: "Minotaur," "*Petite Mort*"
Ploughshares: "Help," "Phoenix," "Snow," "Chapel"
Poetry: "Statue of Eros Without Wings"
Poetry East: "Donor," "To the Pier"
The Quarterly: ``Shower," "Dark Square."
Quarterly West: "Wolf" (renamed "Wolf Trap")
Rattle: "The Boundaries"
Shenandoah: "At the Pair-A-Dice Bar"
Southern Review: "Adoption: Trauma and Recovery," "After Vallejo,'"
        "Gravity"
Southern Poetry Review: "Gallup"
Southwest Review: "Florentine Sunlight"
Willow Springs: "*El Mundo del Oro*," "*El Mundo del Terror*"
Witness: "Fermentation"
Yellows Silk: "Period"

"The Insomniac's Pet Shop," "To Hear the Chorus Sing" also appeared
in *On the Verge: Emerging Poets and Artists* (AGNI/Faber and Faber)
Faber),1993.1993.

Sometimes, alas, all-too-perishable poems outlast friendships. I don't want that to happen here. I would like to thank Marcus Cafagna, Brent Hendricks, Tim Liu, Fred Marchant, Peter Richards, and Judith Taylor for their help on some of these poems. Special thanks to Chris Nicholson and Ron Rubin for being supportive readers and diligent commentators. Also thanks to my poetry teachers in brief summer workshops, especially the core faculty at Squaw Valley Community of Writers, for their excellence as teachers and their goodness as mentors: Robert Hass, Brenda Hillman, Galway Kinnell, and Sharon Olds. And thanks to Ed Hirsch for his inspiration and kindness. Two editors helped to guide, push, and shape these poems: Gordon Lish, with those that appeared in *The Quarterly*, and Jessica Faust, at *The Southern Review*, to whom my debt is more than immense and whose editing was nothing short of marvelous. Finally my thanks to the publisher and my dear friend, Jack Estes, who doggedly wanted this manuscript to come to light in book form.

Dedicated to

Tommy Zankel
1963-2007

and

Joyce Marcus
1933-2010

Contents

I

Dreaming and Waking

We are threatened with suffering from three directions: from our own body, which is doomed to decay and dissolution and which cannot even do without pain and anxiety as warning signals; from the external world, which may rage against us with overwhelming and merciless forces of destruction; and finally from our relations to other men. The suffering which comes from this last source is perhaps more painful than any other.

—Sigmund Freud

No one who, like me, conjures up the most evil of those half-tamed demons that inhabit the human beast, and seeks to wrestle with them, can expect to come through the struggle unscathed.

—Sigmund Freud

Doctor, Please

A militia of crows has gathered in the yard. I know now
    what the symptoms are. One patient took

a hacksaw to his throat then pulled on the rim of his turtleneck
    to expose a virgin scar. Another man recalled his life

as Perseus, forever cradling a severed head. Snake tongues
    on the black sun. The eyelids flutter.

What happened to the party guests who once dressed up
    as astronauts? Most work on Wall Street; one's

already dead. This early morning waking, the anvil of daybreak
    waits above my head. And what about the young

man who claims he's really Icarus and continues to insist
    he doesn't belong on this planet anymore

because he lost his wings near the surface of the sun. Doctor,
    please interpret what the dream voice said:

Go now and follow the owl stone of dawn. Walk to your waist
    through the oil. Moor the blue rowboat

that drifted off from shore. Their feathers, you can touch them
    without harm although they're drenched in chemicals

and heavy from the tar. Your waterfowl are bound to Earth.
    You must find for yourself another way to soar.

The Insomniac's Pet Shop

I have no use for cages.
The gerbils can copulate
wherever they want.

By moonlight, I clean the dead
canary of the birdseed it is lying in,
pluck the pretty feathers—cerulean
and yellow-gray.

With Chopin on the antique gramophone
I savor the skips and scratches,
waltz with the white toy poodle
that sleeps in a wire cell by the window.

In my pet-shop all the fish tanks
are densely laced with algae
no human gaze can permeate.

Buy a goldfish from me—
it's an act of faith.

And maybe, like your own
prayer for rest, you'll hear
the tiny diver
calling you from the bottom.

Gravity

She walks into my office, crying.

                               Not her own pet or that of a relative
or a friend but a dog
she'd never seen until yesterday. Her forehead slumps into her hand
as she recalls how this animal hurled itself over the railing
from the Observation Tower that crowns Mount Tom like a party-hat.

The yowling, the pain-filled yelps—I'd never heard anything like it.

She describes the mound of broken, dislocated bones,
the four splayed legs and bleeding
snout; the laxness of the rescue workers
and the nonchalant comments of other hikers.
"Should have been on a leash." "At least it wasn't a human life...."

                               Returning home to find her mother
halfway through her second six-pack, gazing soporifically
at the autumn dusk that loomed behind Oprah
on the TV screen. So she walked across the road
to visit a male neighbor,
who after sympathetically nodding his head,
thought the best form of comfort was to arouse her breasts.

                               How should a therapist respond to
her clear-sighted perspective,
that if-nothing-lasts-then-nothing-matters, except to say,
if nothing matters—nothing lasts.
Each of us remote in this late autumnal gloom with the image of a dog
sprawled in flight.

My patient remained inconsolable through the hour
while I silently imagined animated dogs falling
from even greater heights
and alighting back on Earth intact.

Scooby-Doo, Underdog, Pluto.
Childhood Sunday mornings lounging on the carpet
beside my sister. Waking in the Sunday dawn
to watch Davey and Goliath. Always one or the other
burdened with regret
for their animal deficiencies and mortal failures.

Next we'd watch The Jetsons,
an intergalactic family with a dog
named Astro, inhabiting a universe
where I often wished to live:
buoyant in a world without gravity.

The Boundaries

...and I must save them,
High fires will help

—John Berryman, "Dream Song 131"

Rebecca the angelic Greek had tributary scars coursing up and down her arms. Sharon with the waist length hair redder than a fire truck and skin Kabuki-pale would light a cigarette, take one drag or two, then extinguish it against her breast. Holly was a sweetheart, her sketchbooks filled with self-portraits in the nude: Pastels with thighs spread wishbone-wide to point where the damage had transpired. "Terror, does it emanate from outside or within?" Fine question Sarah, but why now do I think of Berryman falling toward his end? All these students traumatized by violence and neglect. Liz explained, after years of being groped and probed, she'd watch her hands in dreams turn gangrene—her fingers fall off one by one. How many others have sat squirming in that leather chair, sinking, as they mumbled, "When the ground gave way, I crumbled." But tell me, Mr. Bones, what true words might I utter to the chronically bereft? What about her fantasy: it's better after death? Maureen watched her stepfather drag her mother by the hair like a pull toy. "The guy was really crazy when he drank. A trichotillomaniac in reverse. Even worse, when he picked me up from school, instead of driving home, he'd detour to the woods, demanding that I show him how I eat an ice-cream cone, but to do it on his dick." "When I was bleeding," Jennifer made clear, "my mother's boyfriend wouldn't want to fuck. He'd spit into my face and scream, 'What a dirty little bitch!' Then take revenge on my pet rabbits, slit one's throat and order me to cook it for his supper." What now might I say to offer comfort? Men are more despicable than ogres. Given only a diploma and the language tool, I started to uncover all these girls alive beneath the rubble. Carrie described how her stepbrother would crawl into her bed at night purring like a kitty cat. "He'd lick me head-to-toe, cleaner than a milk bowl, then leave his glue-white puddle on my breast." A doctor resolute in mind. I wouldn't touch you ever, except in dreams and only with my eyes for I too want to heal and live again. Spirit-loss, possession by ghost, symptoms in a diagnostic book. What Henry aptly labeled, the horror of unlove. Lord knows how many times I found you crouching in the scum, huddled at the bottom of a well. It's madness, insists the doctor in his notes, to descend without a lantern or a thread—taking nothing with us but the will. Though Jeanette said it better near the end of one sad session: "Some walls are made of love."

Cutters

Not wood, not stone,
not apple or bread,
not Thanksgiving
turkey or Easter pig;
the cloth she cuts
is her own flesh.
She arrives
on the unit
and I search her
for safety
pins, sewing
needles, pencils
with points,
mirrors concealed
inside compacts.
In group therapy
one patient said,
"a razor blade
is better than sex,
the blood flow
more soothing
than warm milk
with honey."
Cutters sense
the skin as
testament, ruined
palimpsest,
marking lines
like an Etch
A Sketch
till blood
bubbles up
like a hot spring.
If only she could
ripen, peel herself
from her body
I could help;
before she's led,

wrists scrolled
in gauze,
into isolation,
beyond the dead
bolt doors.

Wolf Trap

One forelimb gnawed
through the marrow.

Blood drool in a puddle
on the tongue.

In the hospital dark
calling to the lifelines

on the dove-white ceiling,
wherein the mind

does one go to
release the damaged parts?

Don't cry wolf.
Cry to the bone.

Cry milk.
Or sing

of the un-cracked
tundra that she was.

Snow

Each flake is an old Cape Cod church
with its steeple splintered off.

Still, it is possible
to locate a hymn within.

I was handed a thin
porcelain implement by a man

prepared to die.
He said they are alike

the baton of the maestro,
the white stick of the sightless.

Leaving Park Street Station

Heart wrecked in a dismal year. Too many godless
Boston Sundays benched at the harbor's edge, waiting
for another tugboat's woeful moan, one more broken

vessel dragged in for repairs. In subway glass a ghostly
face appeared: crow lines beneath the eyes, lips cracked
like the scales of a haddock. Deserted by words, I couldn't

even ask myself, how many fractures must the mind endure
before it's finely jigsawed? Nearing dusk, I'd meander
home through the narrow sidewalk chatter of Portuguese

and Haitians: neighbors, teenage lovers, Big Wheels, ghetto
blasters. Though sometimes in the twilight I'd
let myself go beyond the stop at Central Square and ride

the T all the way to Alewife. Arriving at the end, almost
calmed by the steady fluorescent hum. The last passenger sitting
in a vacant car, relieved at not having to go any farther.

The Embrace

The orderlies know he is asking
for this:

to be pinned down
as he bites, head-bangs,

spews expletives,
enraged as they wrestle him

into a skintight suit
like those worn

by divers
about to plunge

backwards
into the frozen sea.

Later, in the staff room
jotting chart notes,

I admire the empty straitjacket
flaccid on the gurney.

Strap me down
under buckle & belt.

                    Hold me.

Courage

All morning the white vans arrive with potted plants
and flowers. I feign having a relative here and tell
the receptionist I'm looking for my younger brother.

"That kid decked out in leather who flew like a giant bat
Above the windscreen of his Harley and now can't make
a fist or talk." Corridors of invalids re-learning how to

walk and swallow as OT's and PT's urge them on: Just one
more step. Lift your spoon. How many heroes in this
one building? How many minds repeating, Why go on?

- Youville Rehabilitation Center
  Cambridge, Massachusetts.

Dark Remedies

> Since our occupation is primarily
> with the failed aspects of life, we
> would have to put away all ideas
> of therapeutic success.
> If I seem to be making the soul
> sick again by such stress on
> pathologizing, I am at the same
> time giving sickness soul again.
>
>   - James Hillman

The day room is a Buddhist shrine.
The morning pills are deities.

Six patients sit with a talk show on
though most are staring into space.

One man stands up suddenly
and hollers—

"Shut up
or else I'll lock you in the closet!"

Another man insists
he's been abducted twice

by Martians, gives a wary,
sidelong glance,

sits tacit
as a fist.

These co-eds, Smith- and Barnard-smart,
interrupted mid-semester from thesis work
on Freud, Muhammad, and Jean Arp.

One woman complains, "My skin is
turning blue like a Picasso canvas,

circa 1902. My fingertips feel icy-cold.
My hands look bare-fist-boxer bruised."

A pair of anorexics on the day-room sofa
whisper about refusing food. One teenage girl
looks defeated. She paces the carpet-quiet halls
in socks. Her nostrils leashed to a feeding tube.

It doesn't require divination or degree
to see this teenage kid is thinking,
"This is all such bullshit."

Another hour of humdrum psychotherapy:
he's male, Caucasian, fifteen,
defiant, a chronic runaway.

Usually it's easy to accept
a session going nowhere.
We have nothing more to say,

though we're both locked up
by the billable clock
for another nineteen minutes.

Maybe, I should willingly agree
and say, Yes, Alex, you're absolutely right.
Time is hell, and worldly life is crap.

❦

At intake, the new admission's face
reveals two befuddled eyes
and an odd, celestial gaze,

suggesting the unsaid
is all he wishes he could say:
"Doctor, What remains

after the self
has been demolished?"

I've seen too many faces peer
down the corridor of mind's

black hole and in a total loss
for words, choke

as if a fish bone
had stabbed the throat.

I understood exactly what it meant:
I am what I fear most.

Ringlets of Bermuda onion,
alfalfa sprouts spooled in airy tangles,

the empty retinas of chick peas,
the scarlet eyeballs of cherry tomatoes.

In line at the hospital salad bar,
staring down into the canisters.

I could really use a double
Hennessy on ice.

Madness curbs the appetite.

Late again for another patient.
Unconscious avoidance?

Could this be my intention?
"For fuck-sake,"

my firesetter growls,
"get me the fuck out of here."

Where else would you like to be?
I ask him and then myself.

His retort, "Anywhere
But this shit house."

Though I for one wish
I was buckled in an Airbus
on a runway headed for Mauritius or Bali.

Twenty-seven session-minutes left.
I still possess an ounce of tact.

With every caustic accusation:
"Uh-hum, uh-hum," I mutter back.

&

Shared psychotic, catatonic,
oxymoronic, hypomanic,

anyone who soars like Mary Poppins.
In the name of peace

I'll grease their eyes, scrub
their minds and won't confess:

getting well's a magic
trick: One day the brain

is in the clear. The next,
mercurial, fickle, sick.

&

Each man and where he dwells,
in a mousehole of his own design,

unwell. Daily group therapy
with seven schizophrenic males

is not remotely comparable
to bachelors meeting up in Vegas.

Laborious this tick-tick-tick.
The wall clock has a terrible case

of Tourette's. "Would anybody
care to speak?

Speak up. Speak
out."

After my patient
hanged himself,
I couldn't rest
for months.
Distress strung
his frayed noose
invisibly around
my neck. From
blood-shot eyes,
I'd watch black
sky become black
day, aircrafts
blink like sparklers
alighting down
the Boston sky
and sidewalk pigeons
grieving. Sky-
scrapers twinkled
like slender bars
of silver 'til
my frenetic mind
went down in
Valium sleep.

I'll be your plumber and your guide
through pipelines of intimacy revived.

Now let's play
a curative game.

I promise I won't make you dance
to the memories of your abuse.

Or have you shape a ball of clay
into your hateful feelings for your father.

The game we'll play
is called, Pass the Miner's Head Lamp.

For fun
we'll search for truth

though we'll need another
prop or two,

especially a top hat
to pull out hope.

Once a week I undertake the role of patient.
My doctor has a fish tank at the entrance
to his office. When he greets me in the waiting
room, I wonder if he's sure they're not piranha?

I don't let on how I'm troubled
by the Miro poster hanging behind his balding head:
spiders, sperm, and raindrops,
red and blue amoebas—entities that madmen claim

lodge inside the cranium. I understand
the dictum, therapist, heal thyself.
But why should my shrink really care what my mother
has in common with my history of lovers?

I think he can see it in my eyes—I'd like to quit
and use the cash for a flat-screen Mitsubishi
or a long weekend in Paris. Subtly, he cautions me:
"You must liberate yourself first, or your life will

amount to nothing but role-play and mockery."
I've insisted more than once, though I might never heal
in accord with the parameters specified in DSM-III,
there are spaces (inside and without) where I can, briefly,

be.

Don't forget the report due tomorrow:
What animals and sorrows did she conjure

from the inkblots? What unblemished insights
did he attain when anguishing these verbal hours?

What are her strengths and deficits?
Describe her capacity for friendship.

Include the tragic tales she told about the boy
with the damaged violin, and incest on the farm.

Once a year for those whose home is "long-term care,"
we offer up an eggnog toast, merriment and cheer.

A choir aloft on high-dose Paxil lines the bleachers
while credentialed men and women, dignified

in trench coats, exhale warmer air into rosy palms
and fidget with sleek leather gloves.

Not often healed and unhealed stand this close together
(almost kin) and (look out from the outside in).

Cold mud, slush, the pill-white snow,
angels hanging upside down, a dozen tongue-less bells.

∽

In a session of art therapy, the patients
are all working hard, praying for

at least a day pass or an overnight
at home for Christmas.

I join them at their lively table
and make a Christmas tree with Elmer's glue

and glitter. The lights on the spruce
burn crimson and beryl as if the remedies

might come. This chill is not
preventable—

it leaks, it seeps
into everyone.

II

The Origins of Blindness

Illusions commend themselves to us because they save us pain and allow us to enjoy pleasure instead. We must therefore accept it without complaint when they sometimes collide with a bit of reality against which they are dashed to pieces.

—Sigmund Freud

The Adoption: Trauma and Recovery

> Far too often secrecy prevails, and the story of the traumatic
> event surfaces not as a verbal narrative but as a symptom.
> —Judith Herman, MD

Below the milk-bell,
floating in the heart-light

alone among the shadows
of your ribs

I wound the bell rope
in my newfound fist.

Hang on
or hang myself and spare us both.

A clear light suddenly fell
on me and I discovered I could

                                        drift

amidst the mica chips
that galaxied your eyes.

Who's your mom? You'll never know
While in the cradle to and fro.

Your blessing and your early curse,
You'll never nuzzle, never nurse.

Now shriek until your face turns red,
My sugar beet, she's probably dead.

Bastard of a lover's tryst,
Have patience, Son, turn loss to grist.

Go forth young soul and part the seas.
Now cure those with your disease.

～

In the dream I am a child unwinding

your ophthalmologic bandages,
searching
        for your eyes.

I unwind the gauze
round and round and round.

Nothing but the same white facelessness.

～

My Mother's Miscarriages

I never saw your river of blood or the two floods
that swept them away from you. Had I arrived
in time I would have stood on the bridge, leaned

over the guard rail, called their unspoken names,
guided their tumbling bodies with my eyes
safely into the ocean where all things are at home

without names. I would have let them live or else
carved their marble tombs with my own whetted rib,
raised thimbles of their ashes to those years of lost

motherhood for I could not offer you an earthly,
healing bread. When the orphan-worker brought me
to your door, you took my name from the New

Testament, as if I could re-write their stories
with my life. Your rock, your church, your indestructible
stone, only time will tow away, not blood, not water.

Help

The Negro came to the white man
for a roof or for five dollars or a
letter to the judge; the white man
came to the Negro for love.
                                    —James Baldwin

How many childhood nights I walked down the dim stairs
to the basement to sit with you and the sound of the rumbling

dryer, to listen to your stories of tyrants and plantations
as you folded with precise care the underpants of my family.

You who knew our human stains: faint arrowheads of feces
and blood. Often during suppertime, an ungovernable sadness

washed over me as you ate by yourself in the kitchen,
after circling around our mahogany table with bowls of string beans

and tin-wrapped baked potatoes. I never understood why you
couldn't join us in the dining room when every morning you

buttered my toast and placed Oreos and Fritos in my lunch box.
After I left for college, it was you who held Mother every afternoon

as she watched her own mother succumb to the hidden grapes
of malignancy, embracing her beside the kitchen sink while Days

of our Lives flickered in the background. Still, Mother insisted
on disguising you in uniforms of baby-pink and powder-blue,

perhaps to subdue the power of your skin, completely ebony,
except for your palms, lighter, the color of milk chocolate.

Shining hands that entered my sickroom at night
with a washcloth that was cool and a spoon dripping honey.

Dolls

With dull gold kernels of hard winter corn spread across my palm I recall
playing jacks with my sister on the hardwood kitchen floor. The bright
spiked satellite of each jack as coveted as antique beads. Once after losing,

I stole her Raggedy Ann and dragged the bulky doll in her calico dress
by the carrot-red braid into the woods to bury her, not knowing what I
was trying to get rid of. Years later, I'd come upon other dolls heaped

in dumpsters, soil-covered in gardens, and one Kewpie beside an interstate
among the black reptilian skins of fallen retreads. Baby dolls all pudgy
and glossy. Teenage dolls with manes of platinum blonde and perfect

breasts without nipples. I've wondered how a child's doll ends up in a gutter,
amputated and dirty, how neglect finds its way into everything,
while their eyes remain so still and crystal-blue, like nothing else on Earth.

Player

There is a game he vaguely remembers that he wants to remember:

A game that girls were especially good at, where an origami
flower turns into a paper mouth which tells the heart's truth.

Pick a number, she'd instruct. Now,
pick a color.

Somehow, he understood, simply by playing, he was winning.

He'd study their fulsome mouths, their downcast, angelic eyes,
the smallest hardest curves of their new
breasts, their hushed joy in keeping secrets, then revealing them.

Though he couldn't comprehend a drop of her theology,
he'd think, Thou art in heaven.

My Sister's Girl Friend

She came uninvited. Self-offering
in flannel nightgown with tiny
sky-blue flowers. No brother at home
to celebrate her flourishing.
I was terrified, too unsettled to touch
her skin as she stepped to the side of my bed
holding the hem of her nightgown
and lifting it up below her breasts
to fan me like a campfire.
Her white smoothness with this
newest tuft more delicate than corn silks,
than seeds of milkweed floating off.

She waited, intent on my attention,
but I was impossible to reach;
so overcome with the desire to touch,
all my brain cells went dark.
Once she was certain that I'd studied
the sprouts of her sexual hair—the birth
of the animal and the woman simultaneously—
she galloped off from my shadowy bedroom
like a young gazelle,
swelling with pride and giggling wildly.

To Hear the Chorus Sing

A man alone in the middle of his bed.

His penis rising because it loves
to rise, regardless of what the man does
or does not love. Shifting like
a compass that guides him through
the forest where he is lost.
Pointing upward to remind him to love
the rest of his body, his small, un-nourishing
nipples, the apple in his throat that blocks
his song like a stone.

As he touches
himself, he defies himself: remembers
the luminous mallard clamping
the duck with his bill, and the dragonfly—
long turquoise needle of light
crazed and sizzling pushing her
in delirious circles around the sky,
coyotes crying from hill to hill,
a barn owl carrying in its voice
the first memory of water.

He senses what
swirls and surges through the stomach,
what dips into the testes and sings
is not the blood, but light reaching
for the farthest walls of space
though never reaching them.
And when desire quiets, he settles
like the sleek crescent moon into daylight,
curling fetal into himself,
holding his animal body like a mother

Rodin Exhibit on the Rooftop,
Metropolitan Museum of Art

Caryatid fallen with urn, fallen with stone.
In ancient Greece these women were motionless
columns upholding the roof, sheltering the world.

Above Central Park set free in morning light,
they trudge one step per century toward
the blockish skyline. Near Midtown, Atlas

steadies the Earth as my father did, hoisting me
above his head before setting me on his shoulders,
not for a view of helium floats or the sunlit treetops,

but knowing his own equine eyes would soon close
and I would become his true periscope.
From the rooftop of the Metropolitan Museum

I was wanting to glimpse Saint John the Divine.
Wide-eyed saints in upright tombs, posed rigidly
in gestures of certainty. No other women here

burdened with the stones and waters of their fates.
While the burghers stood pensively, welded together
before certain death, surrounded by luscious nudes,

backs arched, breasts bronze and firm. Caryatid,
at least you were blessed with a name
like those of birds: small, quick, yellow, fluttering.

El Mundo Del Terror

The violence I dreamt of inflicting on others I discovered
watching wrestling on UHF in Spanish. I didn't care
when a friend's older brother informed me it was all a fake
and a hoax: nose rips, eye gouges, ear twists, body slams,
the use of foreign objects, his baritone voice exclaiming,
Rompe! rompe! le cabeza! I was jubilant with my Spanish ally.
Genuine torture. Pleasure at another's expense. I enjoyed
scorching ants with my magnifying glass, their legs singed,
crisped, curling up, turning into smoke. And pleased to see
the bees trampoline on the guts of a roadkill squirrel.
After college, I read Timerman, Hikmet, Wiesel. Torture
on every continent, a tower of memoirs describing terror
reaching toward the stratosphere. And what of those who
never told their stories? Fingers sausaged off and forced
down windpipes, tongues hacked from the backs of throats,
the snapshot faces in a manila folders, skulls in mass and
unmarked graves. Now I wrestle with other violence within
and around me. That boy struggling on his knees, trying to
press his adversary to the ground, to make him eat dirt, to
take no shit from nobody. No one ever again daring to call
him wimp, pussy. And twenty years later on the office carpet,
a six-year-old, play-therapy patient loads and unloads
a yellow toy dump truck. Welts and scar tissue
inside his anus when he was only wanting to be loved.

To the Pier

The star of our sadness rises invisibly through this coldest daylight
as we walk on hardened snow to the pier. The word *soon*

almost identical to the word *son*, lacking only the o: the hollowness
of exclamation, the mouth that swallows absence.

The o held in cupped palms like a robin's egg, which we fit inside
like a tomb, how father is missing only the r that turns

you into farther, in consonance with over. Language is distraction.
Our silence twines us in a nautical knot. When we speak

of time dissolved by death our blood ropes hold unbroken. This is
how we progress. Here the waves are never frozen.

Bubble

Blowing gently into the plastic zero
he was astonished

how his breath could yield such delicate orbs
finer than Swarovski glass.

It didn't matter that perfection was transient,
for its beauty was repeatable,

effortless as lifting the arm of the turntable and placing it back
at the beginning of the song.

He would stand in the suburban driveway or sit in the backyard lawn,
enclosed in a bubble

of clandestine happiness. Wisps of air emitted
from his lungs

sending the mauve- and lilac-tinted globes cascading into sunlight.
While somewhere in his mind,

in an outlying place, without signage or roads,
he sees himself still

there: green summer
brimming with dandelions and bumblebees,

the round container in one hand,
a blue wand clasped daintily between his fingers.

Bubbles like winged horses rising bounteous around him and he
rising with them.

III

Eros Stricken

Love in itself, in the form of longing and deprivation, lowers the self-regard; whereas to be loved, to have love returned, and to possess the beloved object, exalts.

—Sigmund Freud

Where they love they do not desire and where they desire they do not love.

—Sigmund Freud

Period

I go down on you during your bleeding,
though you insist the fumes that river from your body are the odors
of slaughter, the lamb resigned to sacrifice.
Cramps, headaches, nausea. I bring you
Anaprox with blackberry tea.

In bed when you turn away,
my hands reach out for your dampened shoulders. You say
you're beginning to feel yourself restored by the flowing out.

I see how this letting go
releases you, reminding me why I must enter solitary
spaces whether or not my body decrees me there.
Your blood is deep cherry, plum, cabernet.
Salty roses bloom in the garden beneath you.

Blackberry Night

When I crushed the berries
in my fist,
they bled all over you.

Nipple and navel.
The body knowing
what the mind cannot know:

Faint breezes
skimming gossamer hairs
along your arms.

Globes of pollen
beyond our windows,
floating off.

Leaning over you
in the dark I carry
blackberries.

Each luscious cluster
from my tongue on-
to your tongue,

careful, not to
crush the meteors
of our slow, tangy joy.

Later, breaking them
bead by sweet bead.
The tart juices

dripping in rivulets
over your torso,
a puddle

in your navel.
Our rosary
scattered, in seed.

El Mundo del Oro

"There is a world underneath this world,"
you said. Your breasts dangled over me
like cones of honey. What more do you want?

"There is radiance to what is given form.
Put my elbow in your mouth, my ankle, my nipple."
On lunch break I walk the Hartford barrio,

examine the polished chains in the window,
hoops and delicate zeros of gold laid on black
velvet. Last night we spoke of formal gardens:

Tivoli, Versailles. And when I asked how you
prayed, you answered, "In Spanish, on my knees
and barely breathing in that sorrowful well

within his heart." In the dimly lit park below
your window, junkies, drunkards and homeless
men lie on benches or crawl inside appliance

boxes without a blanket or a coat, while we are
cozy, curled up knee-to-knee, listening as the snow-
flakes pile quietly along the painted chipped sill.

The Happy Sleeping Bed

When my arm reaches out across the lightless air,
my hand alights

         to feel

              if

                   you're

                        still there.

And you're still there. . .

In the Shower

facing you
I feel
as I
once did
years ago
before
the mirror,
dressing up,
believing
I could be
anyone.

Someday
we may
learn to forget
the distinctions
between
tears and other
forms of water,

why the halo
is not meant
to hover
above us
but to
pierce
the body
like a discus:
rapid, gold,
light and
spinning.

Petite Mort

I stand behind her breathing warmly upon her neck
undoing the faux pearl buttons on her charcoal dress.

Two hours ago she buried her mother. Gladiolas
and irises nonchalantly tossed upon the hardwood casket.

She said, "Do whatever you wish, but don't say a word
until I'm finished." I press her down onto her knees

as if guiding her in prayer. She reminds me her mother
was an atheist and when the tumor in her brain

had swelled to the size of a small balloon, she'd say disturbing
things like, "What else is left for me but the shovel

and the worm." Two fingers inside her, circling as she drips
like rain from the wing of a gravestone angel. I know her

pastor couldn't comfort her like this—firing neurons, flashes
of heaven, the surging blood. The oblong hole, she

described as strewn with bits of mangled roots and tear-
shaped stones. "I watched the earth ingest her casket."

In twenty minutes, she insists her pleasure has diminished,
then calmly says, "You should really go." As I dress,

I glance at her. She rocks herself, in cadence
like a motherless crib, a boat released in twilight, left adrift.

Chapel

Laundry strung between high windows, billowy
in breezy light. A circle of uniformed boys

in a courtyard kicking a soccer ball, and someone
upstairs practicing piano. In the dream

a ceramic creamer painted with wild sunflowers.
Streaks of rainbow plumage from small boats

going away. Motor oil. Olive oil. Angels that leap
from the mind onto the chapel ceiling, a man supine

in midair—this is renovation. Now we must wait
for the fish light to surface: a mackerel or a perch.

Rust-colored sausages in a butcher shop dangling
like wind chimes. When I woke, the actual creamer

was bursting with purple grapes, the soccer ball beneath
the staircase, unnoticed, like the world. We say

we have come to gather the bright scales of desire,
though the early fog has swallowed canals and the sea.

It's barely dawn. We should sleep. Somewhere a painter
dips her brush, adding pale blue to the wings.

On the Night She Leaves Me with the Jewels
of Our Sleeplessness

Sanitation trucks at 4:00 a.m. grind north along Eighth Avenue
                                        mimicking the clatter
of an agitated solitude.

Her body asleep beside my body.
                    The arch of her a night-warm sheltering.

The anagram of *need* is *Eden.*
                        Her absence carves a casket out of air.

I wanted her mouth always,
                    even when pungent with chili paste and kimchi.

Only hours ago, I watched
each tear

            drop

            from
             its

            eyelash

                            like crystals from a trembling

                            chandelier.

Phoenix

It was the wrong time and place
to look for resurrection.

Memorial Day, ninety-nine Fahrenheit,
cloudless sky, congested boulevards,
no parking spaces at the mall. Blinding
sunlight and the world on sale.
Always more loss required, always.
And after, feeble gestures to shape
what remains into a marvelous bird.

It would have been fine with me
to know only enough of grief
to raise a wren or sparrow. A tiny
passing song from a little mound
of soot. No, no, says your heart,
make a peregrine falcon, a red-tailed
hawk. Hoard loss until you hear
the last sweep of its wings.

I was told go to this city where
firebirds rush through the air
of burnt light, where imported palm
trees tilt and slump above the sand.
What rises is not a bird or the soul
offered relief, but scents of fast
food burger grease, cod and pollack
frying at Long John Silvers.

It's not your fault your name intimates
magic. To walk these streets
is to walk on coals. I was without her.
I needed someplace to take my ashes.

Minotaur

Was she disgusted by the coarseness of my beard, the toenails
I forgot to clip, or thoroughly repulsed by the pus-red

splotch between my ribs—an old wound from a picador?
Since she seldom spoke, all I could hear was her audible body

wanting to be sated: Do unto me. I am the day lily, and you—
the towering shadow that leads away. Whatever she sought

I can't quite imagine: the ardent grunt, the ravenous horn
perpetually erect. I admit it troubled me when she insisted:

"I only want to fuck you with the lights out." I bristled as any mortal
would, feeling hideous and vile, sensing her struggle to

save herself from me. The self in tiny duplicates in the mirrors
of her irises. The room completely dark. The thread that tied us

to the flaming center reeled back in and severed. An empty space
beside me. She's left the bed to dress. Elastic sounds of bra

and panties, her slowly fading scent. Blue jeans, then a T-shirt
slipped over head, water jetting in the bathroom sink, her wish

that both of us would vanish. My sallow bull eyes follow
the tiny crimson beacon of her burning cigarette.

.

The Affair

I want what I want when I want it.

This is not a song. It is an oak split
by lightning. Charcoal cankering
the wood's core. Chain saws arriving
after, and maybe a friend suggesting

I build a feeder for crows and mourning
doves. The direction of fire is
not for us to know. The wind pushes
wind into the middle of a living room,
or north where snow is falling.

I see Prometheus erotically now.
His bed of warm sand. Tied there.
The cold authority of the sun. Harpies
dressed in evening wear, vicious teeth.

Statue of Eros Without Wings

I think there was no joy
in what was fought for.
Welts where the wings were.
A few feathers of a hen
after the fox has run.
What of the wholeness his body
wanted to belong to? Bone-yellow
hunk of torso bolted to a pedestal.
The radiance used up.
Only his heart lost within stone,
working like wings: that pitiful
flapping as he plummets.

Dogwood Time

I wanted nothing
but to sit, and to breathe within
this white asylum,

cloistered as a sky-
blue Mary.
I'm certain if I hadn't

been at risk of arrest
for loitering, I would
have sat interminably

on the sidewalk on Perry Street,
trying to relinquish
the surges of self-pity.

But soon must come
the nails and blood
and city policemen

incorrigible,
with nightsticks and flip pads
to write summonses.

Archaeology of Water

Ashley left during the last cold days of winter.
The winds were penniless
and the branches pressed against the sky like scars engraved on a living body.

Time refused its ordinary passage.
Hours fallow without measure.
Each day boxed in on the office calendar like rooms without windows.

I was ashamed of being left, having loved, having
been, it seemed, I thought, loved too, then left.

No films, no books, no music.
Only falsehoods unearthed in words.

And a last recourse: to perform an archaeology of water,
alone at the winter river north of Chelsea Piers,
before the stunning moon goes rotten.

Because I cannot extricate the gift from the wound,
I must wait for the moon to open its sarcophagi
and allow me to touch the shining pieces of what was.

Swans, Penguins, Whales & Us

- after Masaccio's The Expulsion from the Garden of Eden

On the body of the blue whale many colonies
of barnacles thriving. Swans coiffure their wings
numerous times per day to keep their feathers
perfectly white. And penguins pass their lives
on icebergs that glow like massive diamonds
in sunlight. This is all I know
of those creatures that mate for life.

When I lived with Laura,
I saw a gradual change come over her body:
her skin becoming mirror, then myself
deranged as in a cubist painting. One eye
on my cheekbone. One eye on my forehead.
Ear on my shoulder like an awkward wing.

The rest was long silences, reaching for
the butter instead of having it passed,
sitting on opposite ends of the sofa watching
Wild Kingdom and Jacques Cousteau explain
how other creatures shielded each other
from predators, adapting once the water
receded and earth was a place we could return to.

Months of strain caused the mirror to flake,
chip, and fall away and I gazed rapaciously
at the skin I loved to stroke, to slip into
my mouth, that she would not let me touch.
There were nights while she snored gently,
I lay beside her staring at the ceiling fan.
The wooden blades cutting apart the nothingness.

How once inside Santa Maria del Carmine
we gazed upon them as they stepped beyond
the Garden, not knowing where to go, shameful
in the light that could not cleanse them. I wondered
to myself, How will they help each other now?
Her hands covering her genitals and breasts.
His hands pressed trembling on his penitent eyes.

Florentine Sunlight

The odors were a mixture that lingered on my calfskin coat:
olives, polenta, hints of musty catacombs, fava beans and grappa.
Men from Ghana set their wares along the Ponte Vecchio:
antelopes, giraffes, and tribal figurines, the goddesses who uphold
heaven. I paused to watch the Arno flow its slightly grimy
malachite beyond the final city bridge, deciding not to pose for
a quick charcoal sketch, for who really needs to see oneself again,
living a second, insentient life as a portrait hung above the bed.

At JFK, I noticed others taking them with care through Customs:
scrolled on beige newsprint, frayed along the edges. Forms
reborn in profane ash, no angel's wings clasped to their backs,
no eye gleam of amazement, no heart gaze of compassion.
It was hell enough to walk among the fountains: all the chiseled
heroes with gull-white scrota. These grim reflections passing
crowded shops. I could never conquer wanting to be loved.

Scarves of silk, pocketbooks and upscale gloves, pastel shadows
varnishing the air, where I glimpsed her in an ancient courtyard:
A girl adorned in primrose crown who stands alone forever. I didn't
stop to consider what desire imagines. What was she but a heart-
beat a stone god can't remember, garlic in the wind, fresh leather?

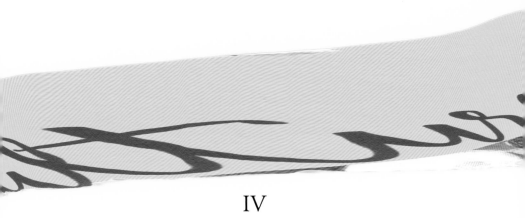

IV

Borders and Crossings

Everywhere I go I find a poet has been there before me.
—Sigmund Freud

Backseat

This is not a joy ride, the upholstery
where I lost my virginity, or the open wind
where I hung out my head to vomit tequ'

Her ex-lover has won her back. The
constant in my eyes. We pass a mo.
abandoned along the highway. Everywhere

a fine for littering. Their voices after lust,
weary yet elated. They take turns driving.
They want to trust each other. I don't ask

to sit behind the wheel. On the highway
it is natural to speak of a future. She glances
in the mirror to check if I'm still there, to say

she needs some distance to clarify things, the way
astronauts try to comprehend the earth by gazing
back on it. They share a sixty-four ounce Coke:

A Big Boy. "You're a big boy, aren't you? Well then,
stop whimpering. You've had enough candy."
Endless tar straightaway through saguaro, ocotillo.

There's supposed to be an oasis with slot machines
and cheap prime rib where I'd gladly hop out.
Sometimes the music on the radio is good, maybe

only because it is familiar. She claims she doesn't
sing, though once, pressed into me
I heard her hum softly. The fool steps to the edge

of the cliff admiring a broken daisy. So what
if I'm just going for a ride, I can doze
and greet the wind. I have the backseat to myself.

Gallup

Along the pocked road snaking scrub
hills into Zuni Pueblo, two dead
mongrels and the windblown hollow
cartons of Budweiser twelve-packs.
Winter on old Route 66, twenty men
loiter outside the Hotel Lexington.
Men with nowhere to go but away:
beyond the rusted boxcars, pawnshops,
the just-for-tourist tepees.

A gusty summer evening in Gallup,
free in the saddle, unencumbered,
quarters for Los Lobos and Patsy Cline.
Warm tortilla like a magician's handkerchief
covers my hands. Make her appear
so we can reminisce over shots of Cuervo.
In the unlit window one *kachina*
grips a bolt of lightning, one waves
a cornstalk in a song for the rain.
I wish the waitress would turn the lights
low and hold me till the flush of dawn
in a slow hip-to-hip country swing.

I didn't buy a concha belt from the staggering
Navajo headed for Lukachukai, nor offer
a ride to his loop-legged friends perched
on milk crates beside the package store.
To know what the drum knows, the eaglet
chained to the ancient roof, new shoot
of a bean sprout risen in fragile triumph.
Where to root? Where are the chains of home?
Just this drum, unaccompanied heart,
days remote from everyone I care for.

༄

Pulling out of Motel 6 at daybreak,
pale faced, hung over, in terra-cotta
light. Towers of sandstone, ticking
dust, tumbleweed migrating nowhere?
A piece of conversation overheard by the pumps
at Thriftway: "Those Navajos got money
for liquor and nothing else."
Two hundred miles from Flagstaff,
scalding coffee, a powwow of ghosts,
the warm, whorled body of a sweet roll.

༄

All morning straight-lined on Interstate 40,
unsure which is destination, which is detour.

The azure-filled socket of Window Rock off 264.
The skyward ladders surging up from Second Mesa.

If only justice was a satisfied coyote who stood
completely still, and wouldn't slither away again

like luck, love, money.

At the Pair-A-Dice Bar

Half the men in Paradise, Montana
are missing limbs.

Their burly forms perched on barstools,
tranquilized by dismantling,

gripping chilled Coors
in the nimble vices

of their claws. One old fellow sings
with Merle Haggard

about scoundrels and outlaws,
while I muse in a rust-red booth,

remembering the sketchbooks of Durer
and Leonardo: a foot, a pure

hand, a luminous torso. The beauty
of all that is partial.

Canvas and Distance

Outside Bozeman we stopped for cigarettes. She spoke of
what was worth suffering for. Only love and art, truth
and song. Wired on No-Doz, we checked-in, in the middle
of nowhere: 3:00 a.m., HBO, complimentary doughnuts at sunrise.
Our room reeking of dead cigars and tropical cologne.

Abbott and Costello on cable TV, then Fred with Ginger
whirling in their elegant helix. She chain-smoked, quoted
Baudelaire, though her icons didn't seem to help her.

Balthus painted felines with human souls. Bacon
painted slabs of beef with a rotten, cosmic glow.
Two partly devoured shapes blasted by cacophonous A/C,
cooling down atop the bedspread, inhaling their sexual decay.
Some frames we were never meant to inhabit.

∽

Driving from Big Sky to Enchantment. All those pretty license plates
stamped out in penitentiaries. Mindlessly calm in the dawn light
east of Abiquiu, where I pulled over, wide-eyed, between beige spires.
Umber dripping russet from inner stillness. At sea in the dryness,
under fish clouds, under bone clouds, ignited by the sandstone flames.

∽

Days after dropping her off in Taos I stood in a thrift shop
in the town where the bomb was invented. A long rack

of wedding gowns on sale near the back: spangled, glittering
like freshly gessoed canvas. How odd, this urge to try one on

and stand before the mirror in drag. The bride of Los Alamos
without a vow to anyone, followed by cow skulls and gorgons

of toxic clouds into a sunbaked plaza in Jemez where children
danced resplendent in plumage: kestrel, eagle, red-tailed hawk.

Fermentation

In the Old World, the workers took
their shoes off to press the Pinot Noir.

There is sadness in arriving before the harvest,
and a bitter taste. The sacrament

of feet stained the color of fresh blood
above me in the cool, white Mission.

The purpose of the grape—crush the flesh
into the spirit, the spirit into endless

longing. Napa, Saint Helena, Calistoga:
early grapes in taut dark clusters.

Migrant workers on their knees
watched by tourists on the Wine Train.

To merely stroll the vineyard paths
keeps us from the underworld,

at least for now. The train ride is nearly
over, and yet, always, this other life:

where we sink among ripened grapes,
vanish into the skins of broken fruit.

Water and the Glass that Contains It

> I am only other when I am myself, my acts
> are more my own when they are everybody
> because to be myself I must be other,
> go out of myself, seek my self among others.
> - Octavio Paz

ABOUT THE HOURS

For twenty miles of dirt road, we followed the sugarcane tractors.
Wilted cornstalks in April heat. A young mother with a pail on one arm
and a newborn in the other. Blackened fields in the distance billowing
bluish smoke. The tour bus pulled up to a dingy cantina. Rhythm
of a woman's hands stacking fresh tortillas. Sun-drained, parched,
a slowness had entered us, and it didn't matter anymore
about the hours.

TIN BELLS

Outside the sugar factory a schoolboy guides a rusted bicycle
by the handlebars past four slim, mustachioed men

walking with machetes at their hips. On the bus
I overhear one American say to another, "There

are no signs here. How does anyone find their way?"
Noontime carries echoes of bells and the shadows of insects

circumscribed by silence. Sunlight in the eyes
of two stone horses, each with a headless rider.

LOS ANGELITOS

The infant coffins on display in Catemaco
are empty, thank God.
But you must know, my friend, that children die here.

Limes, red chilies, oranges and corn, the river
and the well, her eyes
and the clover honey gathered there.

On a brittle wall the faded words: *LOS MANOS
DE RESSURECTION*. The task,

the casket dealer told me, is to live as if
already in the afterlife.

Little coffin, little tomb boat,
even without wind or water, each of us is ferried away.

MEXICAN CEMETERY

I came upon white towers in the city of the dead:
wreaths, lavish bows and tattered lace, red plastic roses
overturned among the weeds, ponderous headstones
of cement cooling in the banyans' shadows. A child's pink
church dress drying by itself on a clothesline.

LITTLE PRAYER

Virgin of the weeping corn,
Madonna of the buried newborn,

Take me
famished as I am

to your turquoise breast,
to your bleeding doves.

SNAPSHOT

Procession of sluggish donkeys, saddlebags loaded with corn.
Rice seed and black wands of sugarcane scattered
on the roads.

Again, the dust—inhaled, tasted, settled on the wide mosaic of pores.
Mud walls crumbling and fallen. Townsfolk
coming and going

from the market before dark with tamarind candies and dolls of felt
and straw. Factory workers, friends and strangers,
young lovers, and a busload

of gringos hoping for the perfect snapshot. . . . Soon the merchants
will pack up and depart with their burlap sacks
of garlic and peanuts,

leaving the plaza empty. For the moment though, it's impossible
to forget the sound of one's own vanishing.
A lantern blown out before sleep.

SUGAR SMOKE

Beyond Los Mangos, warm breezes fragrant with burnt
sugarcane, the russet of drought. Onion vendors lining

the market road. Gold and purple onions, their skins white
as parchment, as the Anglo body. Her spare and simple room:

two plastic chairs, a kettle and a table, a cot, and a calendar
with a painting of the resurrection tacked to the wall.

Her hair, unpinned, torrential, darker than *frijoles*. And like
the sea, the sound of her hairbrush, over and over and over.

VESSEL WITH PAINTED AZTEC WARRIORS

Empty me
that I may be

simply

eyes that gaze upon the work
of love.

The Accordion Players

The poor accordion players of Oaxaca stand on narrow sidewalks
near the plaza, alongside a yellow wall, beside another wall painted
eggshell blue. Stoic in the dry heat, solemn in their scuffed
black shoes.

Tortillas made fresh on the griddle only cost a few *centavos*
and the loveliness of their offered song is free, though the blind
man has already paid dearly with his eyesight, and his nine-year-old son
with truancy from the local elementary school.

The music hums as vendors
pass with whirligig toys, plastic kites and silver bracelets,
a rainbow panoplyof helium balloons.
The musician's daughter in a frilly white dress serenely holds
a red plastic donation bowl and waits for every song to finish.

She follows
anxiously behind me pleading for more pesos. *"Senor, senor, por
favor, me madre muerte."* But I hurry fast away, away from a child's
talk of death over the sun-gold cobblestones.

At the edge of the city, I come
upon a simple graveyard. Pastel-colored angels
shaded by lethargic willows. Is her mother
buried here, I wonder. Has anyone left for her
a single artificial rose?

I return to the *zocalo* at dusk. Another boy is
playing solo. Accordion on his lap, heavier than his own small torso.
"Donde esta tu padre," I ask, after dropping a few coins in his dish.
But he doesn't answer, doesn't lift his gaze to acknowledge
that I've spoken.

He taps the buttons rapidly, fills the old machine
with air. Empties it and fills it, droning on and on with a grave,
ferocious sorrow. *Is your father home asleep? Resting in a nearby bar,
easing his weariness with friends and cold cerveza?*

Although I've shut
my hotel window from the midnight sounds of the plaza, their music
seeps inside me. Son and father playing on through the night,
pressing down hard on the white keys of my bones.

Tasco Triptych

I. MAUNDY THURSDAY

All night I have listened to the rap of metal
chains across old cobblestones, and not forgiven
anyone and not forgiven myself. How dark

must it become? Darker than a bloodstain,
darker than a horse. Death alone and no one
come to comfort the poor clay of his body.

All night the red-mouthed gladiola burn
beside the honey tapers, and the thorns that he wore
are the thorns in which we kneel, then lie down.

II. HOLY HOUR

Propped up in bed beside the scripture of your sleep
I listen to the dogs of moonlit indigo scavenge the trash-
heaped hills. Radiance brocaded on the convoluted sheet
and the flesh spun about your neck equal to the shadow
of a lily. Somnolent dogs in the empty pews outstretched
beneath his spike-pierced feet. Dawn contained within
amethyst walls. On the shores of prayer, I see no one.

III. MADRUGADA

Follow the milk-wax drippings over the silver-gray stones. The whole
moon is a newly minted peso watched
by insidious guard dogs. A mask maker sleeps below

the skeletal faces, while his seamstress wife hurries
to finish the last of the penitents' hoods. It is required
that you grieve alone like Jesus among Roman soldiers,

to suffer with your back turned to the world.
With prayer and nothing else, daybreak belongs
to God only and the shadows of passing birds.

Dark Square

We will all die dreaming something of this world:

its eggs, dust, feathers,
and its body of bread.

                         On moonless nights
the whole house sways
with sleep.

           At dawn, a marlin arcs and wavers
toward the Mexican sun.

Murmuring children pass
through the graveyard gates, carrying little pines.

After Vallejo

> Every bone in me belongs to others;
> and maybe I robbed them.
> I came to take something for myself that maybe
> was meant for some other man.
>   - Caesar Vallejo

᪥

Each morning in Lima near the sea,
instruction or observation:

Beneath the stone head of the condor
gather the windblown petals.

᪥

Each afternoon the scrawny boys waited nearby
as I sipped iced coffee,
                    then hurried alongside me across the plaza,
desperate to shine my rubber sandals.

᪥

The giant bells of Jesus overhead.
The little bells of push-cart men selling
ice cream cones and fresh-pressed orange juice.

The whisperings of school girls and lovers and those
in the silence of exile, standing by themselves,
their backs pressed to sunlit walls as if before an execution.

᪥

Disheveled beggars linger below an urban cross
as if waiting there to witness the actual crucifixion.

I purchase one ripe, unblemished mango from a somnolent vendor.
An offering to no one.

It is heavy in my hands
like something stolen.

❧

What was left of the market at twilight:

A smashed banana, the brittle hairs of coconut husks,
a few scattered kernels of corn.

One gray mule tethered to a rickety cart.
Within one umber dome of an eye: the watery shadow I always was.

❧

Then the rain fell lightly, lighter than the coins in my trouser pocket.
I can't remember when it was I began to turn from others' despair.

It is raining and I remember
the cruel caverns of my ingratitude.

❧

I couldn't discern if it was hope or instruction:
you will write about their shoes

and those without shoes
and those with torn and muddied feet

and those without feet and the man sliced right in half
at the hips who totters on the palms of his hands.

❧

             At the door of the lion
the loneliness was not worse.

Saffron paint formed an oblong
                          of daylight and on

the next street a man
     who insisted,

           you must keep walking
until you see
the horse who carries angels.

       Instead, I met a pauper leaning on a wooden
crutch
begging beside a stagnant fountain,
his left leg amputated

       just below the knee.
Stallion of a man

    mid-gallop

    ♣

The earth holds the edges of a coffin in its darkness.

Amigo, please teach me

    how to cling

to the tin rim   of her halo.

    ♣

One man played accordion by the sea.
Another opened a spout in a coconut

pouring its clear milk into a cone-
shaped paper cup.

White geraniums.
Fallen mangos.

Lime and cilantro as I slept
and when I woke.

Santo Domingo alone on the shore,
indolent, stoic

as the bobbing heads slid under.
I should have gone down, I should

have gone down
on my knees with the others.

❧

I met Blanca on a crowded bus and she brought me
to her home. She handed me the tepid *chicha*, then pointed

where the sunlight fell in the unkempt garden. The red
and green Christmas lights of ripening jalapenos, the dwarf

pillars of corn. I played *futbol* with her nephews, admired
a tattered doll shared by two sisters, though its button-eyes

were missing and left with hanging threads for vision.
With a tin platter placed before me at the table,

the children serenaded a high, soprano grace.
A boiled chicken clawing the air slaughtered in my honor.

❧

In darkness, a glow recurrent in the rooms of lovers.
Golden light on the empty balconies.

Each cobblestone containing a private loneliness.
Each cobblestone set in the earth—a fragment of someone's future
grave.

Men leaning on walls. Men receding
into corners, reading what remains of other people's news,

listening to what remains of other people's songs,
waiting for the moment to put out our darkness with our shadow.

❦

The bus crept torpidly along rutted roads towards Urcos.
In the end you will arrive where you are supposed to arrive.

A ghostly cry appeased at the breast.
Those who slept with open mouths as if they were singing.

Peter Marcus has worked as a counselor and as a professor of psychology, on the college level. His poems have appeared in *Ploughshares, Poetry, The Southern Review, AGNI, Yellow Silk, The Iowa Review*, and several other highly respected literary journals. He currently lives in New York City, but he is always on the move, having traveled to more than eighty countries. *Dark Square* is his first collection of poems.

Poetry Books from Pleasure Boat Studio: A Literary Press

(Listed chronologically by release date. Note: Empty Bowl Press is a Division of Pleasure Boat Studio.)

P'u Ming's Oxherding Pictures & Verses * trans. from Chinese by Red Pine * $15 * an empty bowl book

A Path to the Sea * Liliana Ursu, trans. from Romanian by Adam J. Sorkin and Tess Gallagher * $15.95

Songs from a Yahi Bow: Poems about Ishi * Yusef Komanyakaa, Mike O'Connor, Scott Ezell * $13.95

Beautiful Passing Lives * Edward Harkness * $15

Immortality * Mike O'Connor * $16

Painting Brooklyn * Art by Nina Talbot, Poetry by Esther Cohen * $20

Ghost Farm * Pamela Stewart * $13

Unknown Places * Peter Kantor, trans. from Hungarian by Michael Blumenthal * $14

Moonlight in the Redemptive Forest * Michael Daley * includes CD * $16

Lessons Learned * Finn Wilcox * $10 * an empty bowl book

Jew's Harp * Walter Hess * $14

The Light on Our Faces * Lee Whitman-Raymond * $13

Petroglyph Americana * Scott Ezell * $15 * an empty bowl book

God Is a Tree, and Other Middle-Age Prayers * Esther Cohen * $10

Home & Away: The Old Town Poems * Kevin Miller * $15

Old Tale Road * Andrew Schelling * $15 * an empty bowl book

Working the Woods, Working the Sea * Eds. Finn Wilcox, Jerry Gorsline * $22 * an empty bowl book

The Blossoms Are Ghosts at the Wedding * Tom Jay * with essays * $15 * an empty bowl book

Against Romance * Michael Blumenthal * $14

Days We Would Rather Know * Michael Blumenthal * $14

Craving Water * Mary Lou Sanelli * $15

When the Tiger Weeps * Mike O'Connor * with prose * 15

Concentricity * Sheila E. Murphy * $13.95

The Immigrant's Table * Mary Lou Sanelli * with recipes * $14

Women in the Garden * Mary Lou Sanelli * $14

Saying the Necessary * Edward Harkness * $14

Nature Lovers * Charles Potts * $10

The Politics of My Heart * William Slaughter * $13

The Rape Poems * Frances Driscoll * $13

Our Chapbook Series:

No. 1: *The Handful of Seeds: Three and a Half Essays* * Andrew Schelling
    * $7 * nonfiction
No. 2: *Original Sin* * Michael Daley * $8
No. 3: *Too Small to Hold You* * Kate Reavey * $8
No. 4: *The Light on Our Faces* – re-issued in non-chapbook (see above
    list)
No. 5: *Eye* * William Bridges * $8
No. 6: *Selected New Poems of Rainer Maria Rilke* * trans. fm German by
    Alice Derry * $10
No. 7: *Through High Still Air: A Season at Sourdough Mountain* * Tim
    McNulty * $9 * with prose
No. 8: *Sight Progress* * Zhang Er, trans. fm Chinese by Rachel Levitsky *
    $9 * prosepoems
No. 9: *The Perfect Hour* * Blas Falconer * $9
No. 10: *Fervor* * Zaedryn Meade * $10
No. 11: *Some Ducks* * Tim McNulty * $10
No. 12: *Late August* * Barbara Brackney * $10
No. 13: *The Right to Live Poetically* * Emily Haines * $9

From other publishers (in limited editions):

Desire * Jody Aliesan * $14 * an empty bowl book
Dreams of the Hand * Susan Goldwitz * $14 * an empty bowl book
The Basin: Poems from a Chinese Province * Mike O'Connor * $10 / $20
    * an empty bowl book (paper/ hardbound)
The Straits * Michael Daley * $10 * an empty bowl book
In Our Hearts and Minds: The Northwest and Central America * Ed.
    Michael Daley * $12 * with prose * an empty bowl book
The Rainshadow * Mike O'Connor * $16 * an empty bowl book
Untold Stories * William Slaughter * $10 / $20 * an empty bowl book
    (paper / hardbound)
In Blue Mountain Dusk * Tim McNulty * $12.95 * an empty bowl book
China Basin * Clemens Starck * $13.95 * a Story Line Press book
Journeyman's Wages * Clemens Starck * $10.95 * a Story Line Press book

Orders: Pleasure Boat Studio books are available by order from your
bookstore, directly from our website, or through the following:
SPD (Small Press Distribution) Tel. 8008697553, Fax 5105240852
Partners/West Tel. 4252278486, Fax 4252042448

Baker & Taylor 8007751100, Fax 8007757480
Ingram Tel 6157935000, Fax 6152875429
Amazon.com or Barnesandnoble.com

Pleasure Boat Studio: A Literary Press
201 West 89th Street
New York, NY 10024
Tel / Fax: 8888105308
www.pleasureboatstudio.com / pleasboat@nyc.rr.com

How we got our name:

...from *Pleasure Boat Studio*, an essay written by Ouyang Xiu, Song Dynasty poet, essayist, and scholar, on the twelfth day of the twelfth month in the renwu year (January 25, 1043):

"I have heard of men of antiquity who fled from the world to distant rivers and lakes and refused to their dying day to return. They must have found some source of pleasure there. If one is not anxious for profit, even at the risk of danger, or is not convicted of a crime and forced to embark; rather, if one has a favorable breeze and gentle seas and is able to rest comfortably on a pillow and mat, sailing several hundred miles in a single day, then is boat travel not enjoyable? Of course, I have no time for such diversions. But since 'pleasure boat' is the designation of boats used for such pastimes, I have now adopted it as the name of my studio. Is there anything wrong with that?"

Translated by Ronald Egan

CPSIA information can be obtained at www.ICGtesting.com
Printed in the USA
BVOW030507171012

303179BV00003B/8/P